A Day With Mimi

written by Sabrina Martin Ball, Wyatt Ball, & Lilah Grace Ball
illustrated by Laurie Barrows

This book or parts thereof may not be reproduced in any form, stored in a retrieval system, or transmitted in any form by any means – electronic, mechanical, photocopy, recording, or otherwise – without prior written permission of the author, except as provided by United States of America copyright law. All rights reserved.

Copyright © 2013 Sabrina Martin Ball

www.abitoffbalance.com

off-balance@att.net

 Post memories of your loved ones and share your thoughts at www.facebook.com/ADayWithMimi

ISBN-10: 0615775829
ISBN-13: 978-0615775821

Illustrations & Design ©2013 Laurie Barrows
"Making the World a Happier Place, One Smile at a Time" ™

www.LaurieBarrows.com

Printed in the United States of America

Published in the United States of America

This book is dedicated to Mimi. As a mother, you taught me that love is more important than anything. You gave me strength, laughter, and comfort. You let me complain as much as I wanted. You taught me to trust in my own strength and know no limits. As a Grandmother, you gave my children all your love and you taught them the importance of loving in return. You are irreplaceable.

-Sabrina

Once upon a time, there was a Mimi.
A Mimi is a very special grandmother.
This Mimi was the most special Mimi
of all the Mimi's in the land.
She was beautiful and funny and magical.
She wore magic eyeglasses that helped her see
through walls and even behind her,
so she always knew what
her little grandchildren were doing.

More importantly, her eyeglasses let her see into the hearts of her little grandchildren, so she always knew just what they wanted. She knew if they needed to be tickled, and if they needed juice or some chocolate. She especially knew if they needed a big hug and a kiss.

More than anything in the whole world, this very special Mimi loved to play with her little grandchildren and they loved to play with her.

This Mimi was so special that she was chosen to be a special Mimi Angel in Heaven. She was given a beautiful pair of wings and she soared up into the clouds.

The little grandchildren were sad and cried and cried because their special Mimi was not there to play with them, to hug and kiss them, or give them some chocolate.

Every day their Mimi was still in Heaven and every day the little grandchildren missed their Mimi.

One day, on the way to school, they wondered…..
"What is our Mimi doing today, up in Heaven?"
And in their minds they saw her.

She was hiking on an enormous, fluffy cloud mountain. It was the biggest mountain they had ever seen, with tall trees and huge boulders.

She wore silly red, hiking boots. All the time she hiked, she sang a song, really loudly, to scare away the grizzly bears.

Once the little grandchildren saw her on that mountain, they felt a little better and they went off to school to have a great day.

The next morning, on the way to school, they wondered,
"What is our Mimi doing today, up in Heaven?"

And in their minds they saw her…..

She was camping on the big, fluffy mountain. She had a silly, red camper. All around her were pretty, red flowers. She was roasting marshmallows on her campfire, still singing loudly, to scare away the grizzly bears.

Once they saw her with the silly, red camper, and the flowers, and the marshmallows, they felt better and they went off to school
to have another great day.

The next morning on the way to school, they wondered, "What is our Mimi doing today, up in Heaven?"

And in their minds, the little grandchildren saw her...

Today, their Mimi Angel was in the arctic! It was very cold and she was wearing a silly, red parka. She was playing ball with a sea lion, a walrus, and a whole passel of penguins. The ball was big and red and they all liked to balance it on their noses.

While she played, she sang a song as loudly as she could, to scare away the polar bears.

Once the little grandchildren saw their Mimi in that silly, red parka, bouncing a ball with penguins, a sea lion and a walrus, they felt better and went off to have another great day at school.

"This little light of mine, I'm gonna let it shine!"

Each morning the children decided their Mimi Angel was having more fantastic, amazing, and of course, magical adventures.

Each day was more amazing, silly, and fun.
And each day they felt better and better.

Although they still missed their very special Mimi, they felt better and still loved her just the same.

Little do the sweet little grandchildren know, their amazing, wonderful, magical Mimi Angel is having all those adventures everyday and more.

Not only is she hiking, camping, and playing in the arctic, she is with her sweet little grandchildren every day.

When they are practicing their numbers and letters or drawing a picture, she is watching them over their little shoulders, helping them concentrate.

She has breakfast, lunch and dinner with them, smiling when they eat their veggies, and frowning when they don't.

She runs every race with them. Sometimes even winning!

She helps her little grandchildren build castles in the sandbox, with the tallest towers and the deepest moats.

She especially loves to have sword fights.
She loves being a ninja, a dancing princess, or arresting the bad guys.

Sometimes she is the bad guy because she knows her little grandchildren would want her to be.

Every night, she helps the sweet little grandchildren brush their teeth and wash their faces.

She loves to hear their bedtime stories and listen to all their wishes and prayers.

This very special Mimi Angel, shoos the monsters out of the closet and out from under the bed.

She kisses her sweet little grandchildren's faces and tucks them in.

She tells them she loves them again and again.

Then she quietly sings…..
"This little light of mine, I'm gonna let it shine….."
just in case there are any bears around.

ABOUT THE AUTHORS

Sabrina Martin Ball and her children, Wyatt & Lilah Grace live in Fort Worth, Texas, along with Dad, Jason. They have two Labrador Retrievers, Mrs. B and Dos. Their chocolate lab, Mrs.B, belonged to Mimi (Vivian Martin Rollins) and is grandmother to Dos. Mrs. B is a queen and Dos is just a "commoner". Wyatt attends a nearby kindergarten and loves to practice his ninja skills. Lilah attends preschool at a local church and loves everything to do with fairies, mermaids, and princesses. Sabrina concentrates on ignoring the always full kitchen sink.

ACKNOWLEDGMENTS

This book could not have been written without Mimi's ever present love and the vivid imaginations of her sweet (sometimes sour) little grandchildren.

www.ingramcontent.com/pod-product-compliance
Lightning Source LLC
Chambersburg PA
CBHW060801090426
42736CB00002B/110